FROM THE DEPTHS
OF THE SOUL

From the Depths of the Soul

Collected Poems

BY DENIS PLUMMER

PINYON PUBLISHING

Montrose, Colorado

Cover Art:
Autumn Forest 2537025 © Raul Comino Caballero - Dreamstime.com

Photograph of Denis Plummer by Teresa Plummer

First Edition: March 2021

Pinyon Publishing
23847 V66 Trail, Montrose, CO 81403
www.pinyon-publishing.com

Library of Congress Control Number: 2021930036
ISBN: 978-1-936671-70-0

ACKNOWLEDGMENTS

I want to thank my late husband's colleague, James F. Doubleday Ph.D., Professor Emeritus of English literature, for his astute critiques of "Unicorns in the Sun" and "A Straight and Narrow House" and for invaluable suggestions and moral support while I was preparing this collection of poetry for publication.

I also want to express my appreciation to Susan Entsminger, for her incisive critiques and for editing of my late husband's collection of poems.

Teresa Plummer
Minneapolis, Minnesota

The following poems were published in these journals:
   Encore: "Lido"
   Hoosier Challenges: "Plato, Monet, and the Beast"
   New Earth Review: "Times Foe"
   New World's Unlimited: "Fall"
   The Poet: "Upon Parting," "The Dead Bird," "Poem," "Prothallus"

CONTENTS

A STRAIGHT AND NARROW HOUSE

UNICORNS IN THE SUN

METAMORPHOSES   79

ODE TO THE SEASONS

IRAN

WOMEN ACROSS THE AGES

DEDICATIONS

OTHER FEELINGS

ABOUT THE AUTHOR

Denis Plummer was a poet, scholar, and educator of generous heart and spirit. Denis loved nature and studied flowers and mosses extensively. He used images from nature in unexpected ways in his poetry. His garden was enjoyed by our neighbors and especially by birds, who had their feeders filled all the year round. While at the University of Washington in Seattle, Denis developed a flower identification extension course and would take his students to the mountains to learn more about wildflowers. Denis also liked to have fun and would organize parties, especially garden parties.

Denis and I, Teresa, met in college where I was an international student. What impressed me about Denis was his idealism, enthusiasm and generosity. He invited me on the first date in September to share with him his poetry; evidently it worked, as we were married on December 30, 1966, and have a son who is also an artist. At some point before his death, Denis would tell me "You will have memories."

Denis received his bachelor's degree in Secondary Education with a major in Biology and a minor in English in 1965. He taught high school for three years. Then, upon falling in love with Shakespeare, he pursued graduate work in English literature. Upon receiving his Master's degree from the University of Wisconsin in Milwaukee, he continued his graduate studies at the University of Washington, Seattle, from where he obtained his Ph.D. in 1975 with a dissertation entitled "Generative Poesies: The Book and Child Metaphor in Renaissance Poetry."

Upon completing his Ph.D., Denis taught literature at Jundi Shapur University, in Ahwaz, Iran. Returning to the U.S., he taught English at the University of Minnesota. At home, Denis focused on writing poetry and his garden. Some of his poems were published in poetry journals such as *The Poet, New World's Unlimited, Hoosier Challenges, Encore,* and *New Earth Review.* Unfortunately, Denis' long

1

struggle with his physical health shortened the time he had to devote to writing. It is a great loss to have to say good-bye to such an inspired soul.

Denis intended to arrange and edit his poems before sending them to a publisher; however, his health got in the way. Therefore, upon Denis's death I grouped the poems according to themes, had them edited, and gave the collection a title reflecting the depth of insight and emotions conveyed in his poems.

ON "A STRAIGHT AND NARROW HOUSE"

The house is the one the speaker's father built, where he and his father have lived alone for many years. (His mother is dead.) "Straight and narrow" expresses the path in life that his father has taken, and that the son (who hero-worships his father) tries to follow.

The form is quatrains of four-stress lines, generally without rhyme. It is the form demanded by the content: sparse, straightforward, without ornamentation.

The poems together are a one-sided conversation between the speaker and his father. The father seldom speaks, and when he does it is never about himself or his feelings, and certainly never about his fears. The boy has adopted a similar stoicism. But now the father has died and is present in the house only as a ghost among other ghosts. The young man talks to him, trying to explain to his father and to himself what his father has made him.

At first, the farm around the house appears to the boy as an Eden, except that there is no Eve. But then events disturb this paradise. A neighbor boy drowns, and the boy hears his mother's "terrible shrieking" that night, coming into his room through his open window. A sudden storm destroys the rose petals, and the father screams at the bloodied lying there. The father brings a woman home, and the boy is jealous of her and realizes that his love for his father is no longer innocent. And the house is beset not only by these events, but by the supernatural as well: the "ghost or bear" that left his monstrous tracks by the creek and frightened the boy's father and himself; witches from the moon (and the speaker finds himself riding among them); and the ghosts in the house, so many that he wonders if his father did not build the house for them. And now his father is one of these ghosts.

The first poem in the series foreshadows these evils. It speaks of the "Geraniums so red and doomed," like the rose petals, and calls the house a "sepulchral" grey, with the yew crowded near the steps, as if it were a tomb rather than a house. And the father lies dead inside the house.

—*Jim Doubleday, Ph.D.*
Professor Emeritus of English Literature
University of Rio Grande
September 2018

ON "UNICORNS IN THE SUN"

This audacious sequence challenges comparison to Shakespeare's *Sonnets*. A series of 46 Shakespearean-form sonnets, its topic echoes Shakespeare's: the progress of the speaker's love.

The speaker dreams of his beloved friend among unicorns dancing in the sun. This sonnet sets the image of his friend as someone as rare, pure, beautiful, and precious as the unicorns.

In Shakespeare's sonnets, obstacles, present or foreboded, come between the speaker and his beloved, including the Dark Lady, who seems to have ultimately taken the friend for herself. There is a woman who comes between the two in these poems also, but it is the speaker's wife, and only for a short while (sonnets 3-5). The speaker finally decides that the affair did not happen, that it is only the wife's lie. What really comes between the two is distance and time, and of the two, the speaker sees his great enemy as time, for it is in time that a love can grow cold, that the image of the beloved one can become more and more faint.

Unicorns in the Sun follows the seasons, beginning with autumn in sonnet 10. The most common image in the autumn poems is that of the fallen leaves, sodden with rain, a fit image for loss and mourning. Autumn is also the season of Halloween and its ghouls, goblins, and witches—here symbols for forces that try to separate the lovers. But in the end, all these are impotent; the real enemy is time.

There are no real winter sonnets, for winter would mean the death of love. The two closest are 29, in November, almost winter ("Like tombstones the November trees are cold, / And all my griefs are buried under them"). In 30, even the fear of winter ends with life: "My heart still leaps from frozen boughs and flies."

Sonnet 31 begins the spring sequence, and sets the pattern for most of the sonnets in this series: the contrast between the feeling of spring hope and the speaker's sense of loss ("I fly about the woods with broken wing"), the image of himself as a "lambless ewe." This series also has, in sonnets 32–33, a new image of a grotesque beast that blocks the speaker's memory of his friend. But in 34, for the first time the speaker acts, using his words to send the beast back to "the sea of nightmares."

In sonnet 39, the sequence takes a new turn. The friend's father writes to say that his dear son is dead, killed in war. This news makes impossible all thought of reunion between the lovers; death is finality. The speaker mourns the death in the next three elegiac sonnets. The beloved is named—Ali—in the last of these three sonnets.

In sonnet 42, the sequence comes back to spring—late spring, with all its signs of life against the death of his beloved. But again the speaker acts with his mind, creating living images that bring the beloved back to life, using his art to recall him. And this attempt succeeds, as we find in the final triumphant couplet of sonnet 46: "And death and time I think I have undone, / And now I see the coming on of sun."

And so the sequence comes full circle: back to the full summer sun and the dancing unicorns, and Ali alive again in the middle of the dance.

—Jim Doubleday, Ph.D.
Professor Emeritus of English Literature
University of Rio Grande
September 2018

The Inward and the Outward Garden

PLATO, MONET, AND THE BEAST

The garden I have gardened for so long,
That culminates in flowers everywhere:
Daisies, roses, zinnias, and marigolds,
The lap of summer just outside my door,
I now behold as shadows in my head.

For I can never see nor know again
The faintest blush of pink upon the rose,
Nor can I after soft and gentle showers
Smell the perfume of hollyhock and rue,
Nor taste the honey at the lily's throat,
Nor smooth and velvet iris ever touch.

It is as though a painting by Monet,
Blurring strict line of flower upon stem,
Melding together flower upon leaf,
Impressing vague variety of rose,
Replaces all that in my garden grew.

For one day by surprise I looked
Upon a snake along the ground
Deep in my garden on a summer day.
My eyes met his below his golden crown.
And then I could not see to see the sun,
Drew back into the inwardness of things,
Into the shadows of my gasping brain,
Fled back into the caverns of my skull.

For what delight, my flowers now all gone?
And all that's left: the realness of their bones.

LANDSCAPE

We stoop to smell a branch of flowers
And boldly touch the softest buds of spring
When like a robin our spirit wings
Heavy among the greenest substance things.

And summer comes upon us
With her big belly, unaware,
Fed by the sun and the earth
And all that is above the sun
And all that is beneath the earth,
Vaporous chains of essence
And mortal coils of worms.

Still we do not know, even as we stand mute
Before a harvest wagon, ceaseless toil,
Drawn across the fields by some mechanic brute,
Even as we feel our hearts grow briefly silent
At the first white frost
And feel our brains grow hesitantly numb
When we see the first leaf fall.

Should we not rather on our wind-torn wings
Lift ourselves up into the winter trees,
Beneath which all the robin's songs
In coiled notes do lie,
And see among the deadest branches,
Insatiably more godful than we have dared to go,
The freshest bloom of whitest snow.

EPIPHANY

Last night you sang an aria:
I felt a hundred metaphors
And thoughts that brushed across my mind
No longer felt themselves confined
To utterance in strict metered rhyme
Nor language chained from word to word
Nor logic on itself intrude:
I see a child inside a man:
He might have laughed, he might have cried,
But something strange stood in his voice
Like a piece of cloth hung on a tree to dry
Dripping drops of blood and pain
And joy and sorrow, sun and rain.
I felt the grass grow through my eyes
I heard the trees leaf through my ears
A rose thorn scratched against my heart
I heard the songs of birds in trees
Now loud, now soft, inside of me.
A spider crept inside my head
And spun a cross upon the cloth
Stained with the blood your voice had bled.
I felt myself a child again
Among the flowers in the woods
Deep in the forest of a stream
Flowing, leafing, through my soul.
I felt the need to touch, and yet
I think I felt the need too much.
Today the cloth hangs on a tree
The aria, a fading dream,
And I am puffed with logic now
And feel as leafless as the snow.

WIND SONG

O in the trees today, my love,
Young lusty wind plays on his lute,
Spreads with his windy waves the boughs
And fills the flowers up with fruit.

These woods are ours today, my love,
The apple's hanging on the bough;
It is enough that we are young,
Come be my love and love me now.

It is enough that we are young,
Come let me be the wind in you;
And since we're young, my apple flower,
I'll play a song as soft as dew.

The wind blows colder overnight,
The lusty lover's song is lost,
And on the branches of the trees
He pipes in rage a lovely frost.

A rage that's screaming with the wind
Blows through these empty pipes and bones;
But since we're old and buried low,
A rage, my love, that only moans.

Today where late the young wind played
The apples hang and dry and rot;
The frozen pipes and strings are mute,
And we have paid for what we got.

THE DEAD BIRD

Today I found a broken bird
In leaves upon the mud,
And on the leaves around the bird
I saw two drops of blood.
"This bird has fallen from the moon,"
I thought with desperate start:
It is the bird that once flew round
The palace of my heart.

I TRAFFIC MYSELF IN FORM

Inside the garden of my mind
My soul turns into flesh and form
And is too heavy for the halting
Beat of my soul's wings to bear.

Like Icarus in his high ecstasy,
I traffic my soul in form,
A soul that can't begin to bear
The fleshy weight of it.
It falls, panting and gasping,
Like a wounded Pegasus.
Blood trickles from its raw mouth.
With limbs and brow of flesh,
It lies dying under a white lily.
The petals of roses fall.

I can hear the low breathing
And the slow drift of petals.
I see my garden grown awry.
Boggles my mind—oh, this my soul!
Here a bruised hip, a scraped knee
There a cracked skull and broken wings:
A cold, grey form that I must bury now
Before the birds swoop down to feed
And pluck out my soul's eyes.

AT LAST

A thousand wounds and after all
Into your garden I have crept.

One last turn toward innocence,
One last turn away from death,

Like a wounded soldier come to cry
Like a sore lover come to sigh.

There is a slight autumnal breeze:
I hear it purring in the leaves,
As one by one the petals fall.

Just so does my wound bleed,
Collecting into pools of petals.
I cannot tell the petals from the blood.

So when I die,
My skin and bones,
Let them not know
The grave from grass.

One last turn away from death,
One last turn toward innocence.

THE CARDINAL

It is not easy lying under ground.
The nights come on so cold, no one around.
I cannot reach to touch another hand.
It is not easy being so alone.

Sometimes I hear a cardinal in the trees,
Blessedly singing his winter song.
Sometimes I feel a shivering to the bone.
I dressed for death. Why didn't he for me?

PROTHALLUS

These fragile heart-shaped leaves of fern
With roots that press us to the earth
In silver fungal threads or moss
Transmute us to our royal birth.

This mossy film of dew and green
That grows upon the dead cock's wings
That grows upon our weathered bones
Will be the leaves of many springs.

So go to sleep, my lovely child,
And let the spider spin the moon
While we become the queen and king
Of this fern-leaf rock forest wild.

THE OUTWARD GARDEN

The beast that lay couched in the garden
Has sprung, and we flee from each other.
We turn inward to ourselves again,
Eyeing the beast among the roses.

Innocence that stood within our hearts
As gentle as hyacinths
Has stumbled and fallen and lies
Among the flowers for the beast
To feed on, to eat to the last bone.

The blood drips from his mouth,
Staining the grass and petals and leaves to red
In the garden from where we have fled
Each other to turn to ourselves again.

To be alone soon becomes as familiar as winter.
The beast has engorged itself on our pleasures,
And that is the end of our pleasure.
Love was a little bird we talked about now and then,
And the beast has eaten our tongues.

FALL

The leaves are falling from the trees
With drops of blood, or torn with shrieks,
With wind they gush in crimson flow
Swelling the woods with a flood of leaves.

A little month ago, my love,
The leaves were green and we were young.
We slept upon the mossy bank
Of this then summer pool of moon.

Tonight crouched cold beside the pool
We shiver in this gnawing wind
And hear the branches of the trees
Tear at our hearts like hungry ghouls.

THE INWARD GARDEN

Upon the eve of winter,
I draw into the castle-
   garden of myself.

I go inside.
I close the gate.

Image after image
Comes to me
   of tulips and daffodils,
      dogwood and willow,
         meadow larks and robins.

As though someone
Had gotten inside my head
   and painted scenes of spring,
      except I touch
        and smell and hear.

Look, these flowers in my hand!

I lie and dream.
I do not sleep.

And if I cry,
My tears are like red tulip petals
   scattered near the castle wall.

And if I do but close my eyes,
I try to keep away the snow.

LEAVING

Flowers bloom again.
Winter snow is gone and my
Heart half warm, half cold.

June bursts a thrust of roses,
Petals bleeding in the rain,
Silent on the thorn.

Leave the hush of love.
All flowers bloom in wind;
They gather sunshine.

Forget the night of love.
Cherries still bloom with flowers—
They know more of hours.

Give me all your love.
It asks no single question
Nor a flower in the rain.

A chill came on me—
Was it the cold or the wind
Or a thought to hide?

Ah, this autumn waste!
Where are the roses now?
Petals, perished song.

If I think of you,
The elms would drop their greenest
Leaves and I would cry.

SHE

If these sweet flowers turn to this,
Then why should I, a man, despise
What she for me has like devised?
To be a clod of earth again,
To lie in peace among the rain,
To be a fluid rush of rain,
At last to find myself in tune
With all the seasons of the year.
But still a single thing I fear:
These sweet flowers my eyes will miss.

DIONYSUS

The grape leaves falling away:
    They fall from the vine
    That fell from the tree
        in the night of the wind
        that will blow them away:

They will be blown away
    The grape leaves that fell
    From the bough of the tree
        in the night of the wind
        blowing leaves away.

They will be sipped into earth away.
    Don't spill your wine.
    The grape leaves are falling
        in the night of the wind;
        I can swim … away.

MOONY

These leafy flowers on the trees
Are lit by moon and spider web;
My love, we're lit by the same light
Dancing in this stormy breeze.

And as we dance we hear the sound
Of thunder rolling through the leaves.
Of thunder from the white-winged cock
Dancing on his mating mound.

The woods are filled with his call.
He struts beneath the lacy ferns,
He pecks the feathers of his wings,
He flies into his henny flock.

The clouds are floating into moon
Like witches riding on their brooms;
The spider light is going out.
My love, the storm has broke too soon.

My milky pool of love is spilled;
The cock is huddled in the bush;
This storm has torn our lovely flesh.
My love, with rain your eyes are filled.

The moonless, leafless flowers lie
Upon the ground the maggots churn,
And all that's left of spider light
Are ashes of a fly.

SANCTUARY

1

Through the attic window
Icicles hang as cold as snow.
I keep him in the cellar now
Next to the bushel of ashes.

Grandfather hangs on a rusty nail;
His face lies buried in the dust.
Nailed to the wall, crooked he clings
To the dust of his own place.

2

Let me believe in trees again,
The fresh wet of the wind and rain,
The trickle of water over rock
Like someone crying in the leaves.

The yellow gust of wind in trees,
The lusty heaves of cloud on cloud,
And yet a little while in these
The bulging buds of lily flowers.

3

How blue the jays against the white snow!
How red the sun below the white hilltops!
If there were thunder in the snow
How gray the limbs of emptyhood!

Wrapt in roots and busted pots
Down three tangled flights of stairs
He waits to feed on these bent bones
And ravishes himself all day.

STORM

Bulging thick with heavy cloud
The sky lay sinking into night;
Beneath the storm the rush of blood
In jets and streaks across the sky
Spread gushing from the tortured sun.

All night it snowed upon the hills
And meadow bloom of daffodils.

The deed that's done is not undone;
Nor who could throw a question why?
Some wore a mantle, some a hood
To hide their faces puffed with fright,
To keep them from the icy shroud

Of snow that lay upon the hills
And meadow blooms of daffodils.

PICKING BLACKBERRIES, SHE SAID

We are not so beautiful or young
As when that summer in the leaves
We picked blackberries
And you were scratched from head to toe
I licked your wounds,
Nor when in yellow light of dawn
We lay upon the moldy earth.
Children's voices shouted
Through clusters of lilacs
From root bottom up.

This autumn eve the birds
In sacred silence cluster in the leaves.
The air as thick as honey
Pours down our steaming flesh.
A sudden blast of wind from the south
Has brought the heat inside our house.
Berries cling to bush.
We try to find our wounds.

SILKEN CHERRIES

I spun my silken web today
In silver after silver silk
Upon the blooms on cherry trees;
Spun silver threads among the blooms,
Among the blooms late hung in June.

Then saw the florid sun go down
And woke to see the silver threads
Shine golden in the rising moon
And screamed to see upon the trees
The bleeding cherries hung in doom.

SONNET

When with all suddenness upon your cheek
The lilies blush and blush themselves to rose,
Then does my leafless soul in your heart seek
A hidden bed in which I might repose.
When those fresh eyes burn with such golden light
That all the leaves are filled with pearly gold,
As when the moon on some long winter night
Will stoop to kiss the hills all snow and cold,
Then is my soul like those same hills in spring
Which, changed to musk and dew and leafy mold,
Contain a billion spurts of wriggling sting,
A ram upon those hills that seeks its fold.
Sweet love! You do transmute my thoughts to wings,
And all my heart leaps to the leaves and sings.

A Straight and Narrow House

1

This is the house my father built.
It is a straight and narrow one.
Against it winter storms have blown,
And on it fallen summer rains.

Tall and slender windows look
Upon a garden that has aged.
And here a door that's half ajar
Lets in a thin and narrow light.

Through other windows I can see
Geraniums so red and doomed.
They look like blood against the panes.
They look like someone screams and screams.

This house is a sepulchral grey.
It is so bleak and made of stone.
The yew are crowded near the steps,
And roses here no longer bloom.

The night my father died at home
I crept into the attic there.
The spider webs were all askew
As though a soul had flown through them.

The night my father died at home
In this house that he had built,
I curled up so close to him,
A thing I hadn't done in years.

For hours I lay in that great bed.
His eyes were closed, his hands were cold.
He did not breathe, he could not speak.

Most certainly his soul had left.

That form of flesh in that great bed.
Inside this house that he had built,
Lay like the path his soul now tread,
More straight and narrow now he's dead.

2

On this a day in early Spring,
Just when the ice has left the lake,
The grey Canadian geese are back,
A wood duck, mallards, coots swim by.

Only the north side of the woods
Still keeps an icy path to walk,
But still the blood roots blossom here,
The scent of mayflowers fills the air.

And where I find the Pasch flower bloom
I look for blood upon the ground,
But only find a spider's web,
Held in its silk the native sun.

Another season must come by,
And I am glad that it is Spring:
Still like a lover I will call
Your name among the tender leaves.

3

The apple orchard on our farm,
Dressed in pastel elegance

And here a blush of brighter pink,
Prefaced the coming on of leaves.

When gradually the petals fell,
There now was fruit where blossoms were;
The bridal dress lay on the ground,
And through the leaves I saw the sky.

Like a Persian palace dome,
The blue sky arched above the trees,
And like a priest or prince I knelt
And faced the early rising sun.

But here there was no sacrifice
Of blood to please a sober god;
Was just the rent in Nature's gown
Where I had knelt to pray to him.

4

Ours was a house without women;
No mother, no sister I knew,
Except for the portrait of Mother
That hung on the living room wall.

But once, my father spoke of her;
He stood, his eyes in pools of tears,
But kept his voce with measure calm.
"She was a fine woman," he said.

And, oh so beautiful and fair
Her lovely portrait graced the wall;
Like cherries were her parted lips,
Her hair was golden as the sun.

Her eyes an even shade of blue,
Her cheeks like roses bathed in pearl,
Her teeth so white and comely straight,
And sure I loved my mother well.

5

When the last days of Winter fell,
Foes insidious on the hills,
And the brave soldier Spring returned,
Our farm in jubilation sang.

For there were birds attending him;
Their songs were heard from every tree;
And like a soldier to be home,
He did not sleep the whole night long.

But he told stories where he'd been;
I heard him in the birch and oak,
How knight-errant he had passed
The underworld which dragons kept.

Or so I thought I heard him tell,
Where does the Spring when April goes?
Or if him as a brother loved,
Sure I was glad when he came home.

He lay within the willow's arms
And made her big with rich increase,
This soldier who great battles fought
And now returned, embraced our farm.

Yet like a soldier off he was,

When we had planted all our fields,
To journey in the nether world
Till his bright days come back again.

6

On this, the porch side of our house,
I like to muse and capture time,
And recollect the golden days,
The streams of light about our farm.

The cows that in the pasture lay,
The sheep that never left their fold,
The rooster out among his hens,
The gentle mare with her new foal.

Radiant these in heaven's light:
The mist that rose from Partridge Creek,
The ferns and moss along its bank,
The tiny twin-flower there that grew.

Had Virgil strayed down to our farm,
Such pastoral lays he would have sung,
And easy had his route then been,
Our farm so near the Milky Way.

I recollect one summer day,
Was in a clearing in the woods,
A yellow lady-slipper fair
Adorned with pearly drops of dew.

In ritualistic circles stood
Albino Indian pipes so rare;
As if by magic half entranced,

Cross-legged, I sat next to them.

Though many years ago it was,
It seems as only yesterday,
Drenched in the light from heaven sent,
The woods, the fields, the animals.

7

Almost as though he'd stopped to rest,
I came upon my father there,
In the small pasture next the Creek
Which afternoon still held its dew.

He looked for all the world alone,
A man adrift upon the land;
He may again have Adam been,
So fair and innocent he seemed.

On him I did not mean to spy;
I watched him doff his heavy clothes,
Then slip into the waiting Creek,
As though it might have been his bride.

When he had swum a little while,
He stepped onto the pasture green;
More like an angel seemed he then,
As though the Creek had purified.

Like a man by Angelo,
His curly locks lay on his brow,
Nor could the ferns but half conceal
His flower in the locks below.

My father was a godly man,
Of this I'm sure I've said before,
And more like Adam that day seemed;
I never mentioned it to him.

8

I see the pale look on her face,
Our neighbor bent over her boy,
Who drowned in our lake that Summer;
But an hour, he was alive.

I hear the soughing of meadows,
And the sobbing of trees,
And the storm that came up quickly
As the sun hung over our farm.

That night the terrible shrieking,
Like a rabbit caught by a hawk;
It came through my open window
And heavy as stone to the floor.

Or a mare painfully breathing,
Softly panting and near my bed;
So heavy and wet on the floor,
Then the shrill, shrill shrieking again.

What horrible shape beside me,
What human pain near to my bed;
She who will always be lonely,
A child who will always be dead.

This garden that my father grew,
With hollyhock and roses fair
With tulips and with daffodils,
Lies overtaken now by rue.

To this garden often we
Would come to rest within the shade
Of gentle oak and birch and elm
And I a child just half past three.

His hair it seems was always grey;
I never knew how old he was,
But knew he lived a long, long time,
And always he had time to pray.

The thunder from the hills came down
On glorious Summer afternoon;
The wind and rain then started in
And stole away the garden's gown.

Those petals lying there so red
Upon the lawn I still can see,
I do not know why father screamed;
I guess he thought the roses bled.

From that time on my father stooped,
His back appeared as half undone;
The rain it stopped, the sun came out,
The clouds along the sky regrouped.

If only glorious Summer days
Had stayed within our garden there,
My father may have never known

But lived among the sunshine's rays.

Whatever there was to be known
Of petals fallen on the lawn;
My father never spoke a word,
But ever can I hear him moan.

10

The leaf ungirded in the elm,
The tender bud on apple tree,
The weeping willow by the Creek
Attend the coming of Spring.

And all about our little farm
The birds in joyful chorus sing
Along the meadows and the woods
Their matins of the early morn.

The wrens return to their old home,
Husband and wife in modest dress;
The oriole, more brightly clad,
Shows off the mistress of his house.

The birds, they teach me how to sing;
The willows show me how to weep;
That I might wipe away the tears
And write for you an epitaph.

For you, dear Father, do I write
This elegy for love of you,
And with my comrade creatures sing
Your praise among these kindred trees.

Your name on every single leaf
I will inscribe with this bright quill,
Until at dusk the cows come home,
And I must milk them in the barn.

11

If after all these years since then,
And I still live upon this earth,
What yoke to hold me like an ox
Could hold more dear than this our farm?

Where I was born and where you died,
Count not the years, send them back home,
This pristine garden that was ours,
The fields, the orchards, and the woods.

This was our homely paradise,
A pasture here of grass and cows;
We helped this fecund land to bear
The crops that kept old Winter out.

If after all these years your death
Still makes me full of angry grief,
To what god as suppliant
Should I bear this slender wreath?

Nothing returns your eager voice;
Nothing returns your gentle hands;
Still, Father, will I linger here
Until this shade transform to light.

12

That was the Spring I came so close
To the blue heron at the Creek;
I must have walked a mile or more
The narrow path to where he stood.

Close up to him he stood so large,
So fine a bird I'd never seen;
I saw the sun set with his eyes,
I've never heard blue herons sing.

Or is he of a silent song,
The grace and beauty of his wings,
The tall composure of his form,
His head held high above the Creek?

I could not move, I stood transfixed;
My eyes were riveted to his;
In him I thought I saw my soul,
Or so it seemed as I watched him.

Then gently lifting from the Creek,
The great blue heron rose and rose;
He beat the sudden sky with wings,
Then disappeared into the night.

13

Whenever I see a swallow,
I remember our house on the hill,
The Summers we worked together,
And the evenings of whippoorwills.

The meadow lark on the fence post
Behind our magnificent barn,
And the cows come home in the morning
From all night long in the field.

And here an occasional robin,
With four blue eggs in her nest,
Ours like the ark of Noah;
That Summer our neighbor's boy drowned.

It was you, my father, who found him,
It was you who pulled him ashore;
And always I will remember
That dolorous look in your eyes.

Yet there were the other Summers,
Of these, dear Father, I know,
Of laughter heard in our house,
Of green fields of clover ad corn.

Of the hill tops red with sumac,
Of the flowers near Partridge Creek,
Of fireweed and mallow, and blue bell,
With these I content my mind.

Still was there always the sorrow
From each other we kept unknown,
Of swallows returning to Eden,
The death of our neighbor's boy.

14

And circumcised my father was;
I only saw him once and knew,

But could have told it by this house
He built by hand some years ago.

Every joist was cut and trim,
And every beam and rafter fit;
Quite pleased he stood when he had done
The fireplace along one wall.

And every rock he split by hand
To let the face of stone without.
I see his arms around the stone;
My father was a lonely man.

The time I knew that he was clean
Was after we'd been working hard
Out in the fields among the corn;
We stripped and bathed in Partridge Creek.

We stripped and bathed in Partridge Creek,
And then we ran the journey home;
I heard my father say, "My son,
Let's pray tonight the corn will grow."

This is the house my father built;
His face perhaps I'll never see;
I only know that he was clean
And sleeps among the fertile fields.

15

Sometimes the lightning flashed so bright
The haystacks stood like sentinels;
The thunder ran across the hills
And disappeared into the woods.

And near the window in the rain
I sat and gazed along the fields;
I saw my face in rain and glass
Looking through distorted mirrors,

As though a ghoul looked back at me
Since down the glass the face did run,
Or some wet spirit in the storm
Attempt to rise and fly again,

And never made it any sound
That could be heard above the rain,
Except it might have scratched the glass.
I do not know, I cannot know.

It wanted in, I kept it out
By pulling closed the curtains tight;
Too many ghouls rise from their beds
In such a storm on such a night.

16

When the carnival came to town,
The gypsies stayed down in our barn,
Up in the loft where it was warm;
They never did us any wrong.

Gay gypsy music did they play,
The girls wore bangles on their arms,
The men danced with a gypsy grace,
And men and men and girls embraced.

The lion tamer, brave of men,

And solitaire, a banjo played,
While long the fortune teller read
One's whole future in her glass,

Till circle of the dance gave out;
They climbed into the warm hayloft;
The gypsy lady of the glass
Put her crystal ball away.

The fire they built in embers lay
On lawn between our house and barn;
I heard the screeching of an owl;
Next morning, all the gypsies gone.

17

Sometimes I of my father write
As though my lover he once was;
For it is true I loved him much
And cherish thought that he loved me.

He was a curly dark-haired man,
His eyes were steel, his shoulders broad,
And ladies of the countryside
A little blushed when they saw him.

Attend them Father never did,
And as a child of that was glad;
I wanted all my father's love,
And Father never wanted them.

Alone my father kept this house
And the garden and the well;
Him I helped where I was able;

Ours was a house of innocence.

But once he brought a lady home;
I heard them in my father's bed;
Could not believe that Father would
Sully his and Mother's room.

For days I hid about the house,
Would not come out until she left,
And when she did I followed her
Off the farm, I hoped, for good,

And pricked her heart in effigy;
The doll lay scattered on the floor;
I thought our love was innocent,
But after that, it never was.

18

November comes upon me too aware
Of the brief glimpse of summer that I saw.
With you away this house is like a tomb.
Most days I stay in bed till after one.

By five I start to work around the house
And polish lamps and tables of their dust.
I cannot eat because you are not here.
Half paralyzed, I sit so straight and tall.

At times a chill creeps in and through this house.
I hear its bones climb up the basement stairs.
I feel my own bones narrow at the sound.
The autumn winds are always at my back.

There was the night some shadow took a form
Outside the kitchen window looking in.
I pulled the curtain shut across his face
But hear him still outside the window breathe.

This night the elms are all robbed of their leaves.
This night this house is empty without you.
I hear the rain like tears fall on the roof.
I see your footprints in the silver grass.

And who will fix the shutters in the Fall?
And who will plant the garden in the Spring?
This house still echoes with funereal words,
And every word of grief makes this house cold.

19

I remember the snow that fell so deep
In mid-December and the hills
That lay in splendor half transformed,
The hills on which I took my sled.

And Partridge Creek a slender stream,
It lay so quiet in the snow;
A cardinal swept the branches off
A limb that hung down to my head.

Was then I saw him standing there,
A ghost that stood within the trees;
Like thick, black threads the branches hung
And pressed against his bony face.

He was the ghost that kept our farm
On Summer nights among the leaves,

And often heard him brush our door;
And then how pale and thin he looked,

For never came so close before
That I could see his yellow eyes—
And saw the jaw drop of his skull,
The hollow look of one half starved.

Nor did I wait to hear him speak
But ran as quickly as I could
Across the hills, back to our house,
And safely in, I locked him out.

Sometimes I recollect that day
The ghost that sprang from Partridge Creek,
Just as the sun sank from my sight,
The sunken eyes so all aflame.

In Summer, Winter, Spring and Fall
He followed me about our farm,
Yet never saw his face so close,
Framed in those branches, sun and snow.

20

The swallows return to the barn
To nest, and the cattle are gone;
I look from our kitchen window
To hills that are springing with green.

Here are on a quiet forty
No tiller, no tractor, no plow;
And the fields, they all lie fallow;
They have not been planted in years.

Still comes with returning swallows
An image of you in my heart,
How we rose at early sunrise
To tend to the cows and their calves.

But now the barn is so empty,
Except for the swallows that nest,
And the odors of hay and cattle
Barely linger after the years.

Yet still I see you at sunset
Coming once more home from the fields,
And your supper I have waiting,
As I have for the last ten years.

21

It could have been a ghost or bear
That left its tracks near Partridge Creek,
Up the trail where the ground was wet
And shaded by the maiden ferns.

Which one, my father never said;
"If it's a ghost, there is no fear;
If it's a bear, it ran away;
Come, son, forget the ghost and bear."

But still I knew my father well;
For a brief time as still as stone,
And dark hair on his arms stood up,
The quicker breathing on his lips.

And never saw a track so large,

Not deer nor cow, for there were claws,
As on that day near Partridge Creek
I felt a tremor in my bones.

22

The shadows creeping up the wall
Are filled with moon as evening falls,
Are filled with witches from the moon
Who ride tonight upon their brooms.

They strip their rags away from bones,
Their green eyes flit across the grey;
The witches on this night have flown
To gather men made out of clay.

Their knives are wet with snake and goat,
They toss their heads on wrinkled throats,
And slit my hanging outstretched tongue
Bleeding screams when I was young,

And walked upon the clover hills,
And sang a song of Jack and Jill,
Till toads as big as dragon heads
Came creeping from those hills I fled.

The moon, full moon, behind the trees,
Smooths the wrinkles of her sleeves;
I ride among the witches now,
Above the fields, above the cows.

The moon that slept upon my bed
Has crept behind the trees and bled,
And all her silver streak of sleeve
Hangs on the branches like a leaf.

Unicorns in the Sun

1

Last night as I lay sleeping in my bed,
I saw a field of dancing unicorns,
The beasts came dancing through my drowsy head,
And bright the sun did glint from off their horns.
Among the herd of them I did espy
A handsome youth robust with curly hair,
He was a man but stood with boyish eye,
His shoulders broad, and how his cheeks were fair.
All night he played among the dancing herd,
He gamboled and upon their backs he rode,
And though I never heard him speak a word,
His bright clear image did good tidings bode.
Among the unicorns 'tis you, good friend!
Then I awoke, and all my dream did end.

2

Today all thoughts of you return to me
Although I have not seen your face in years;
I know that once together we were free,
And laughter flowed where brooks now flow with tears.
Eleven seasons come and gone but yet
I still can see you walk among the leaves,
I still can think on times when we first met,
Your smile, your touch, where now my sore heart grieves.
But for a little time we were sweet friends
And though we hurt at times we did embrace,
A memory of you today that lends
An instant joy that time cannot erase.
So let time come upon us year by year,
So long as I can think I will not fear.

3

If ever I did do you any wrong,
By word or act, I beg, then pardon me;
Accept in recompense from me this song,
And let us once again two close friends be.
Now let us end at once this bitter strife,
This fray between two stallions on a hill.
Whatever went between you and my wife,
'Twas no big thing, if you'll forget, I will.
Our friendship always dear to me has meant
A sunny garden full of freshest bloom,
A kinder hand that brushed away the scent
Of time upon the leaf of darkest gloom.
If ever, friend, me in your heart did hold,
Rise up, and join me in our bond of gold.

4

If ever I should turn to you, my friend,
And know full well that you will me betray,
Our friendship dear once more might find an end,
And what should we each to each other say?
Rude silence leaves its stain upon my tongue,
My heart would speak but has no tongue to tell;
I think upon that poet wise who's sung
Of this same theme and knows his songs too well.
And he is kind but cannot match my grief:
I have a friend who stole from me my wife.
My heart hangs trembling like an aspen leaf,
Betrayal framed our friendship into strife.
Today I lean upon a withered cross
Accounting to myself a double loss.

5

Of all the lies your serpent tongue has told
No lie has ever been so coarse as this:
That you with my dear friend were overbold
And took him to your bed of lover's bliss.
That you caressed his body while he lay
His head upon your lap, you sang for him
And with your tender touch did you repay,
My golden rings upon your fingers slim.
That you, unfolding like a crimson rose,
Would take him to your deepest lavish fold,
And then did say that it was he who chose
The icy touch to make our love grow cold.
But this, my dear, was purely in your head;
My friend, he never crept into your bed.

6

You lay with hands at rest behind your head,
Your cheeks were pale, your lips were thin and blue,
You lay as if you weren't asleep, but dead.
Half scared, half numb, I stood and stared at you.
I heard a fly buzz gently round the room,
The breeze blew through a broken windowpane,
There was a sense of silhouettes of doom,
A sense that what I'd do would be in vain.
For what, dear friend, as you lay seeming dead,
Could I do now but only stifle screams?
You lay so still and quiet on the bed.
How many times I dreamed these nightmare dreams.
For if we love, then love has made us choose
To love the one we dearly fear to lose.

7

There would have been a time for cutting off
Our friendship and our love and all our dream,
A time for us to look at Time and scoff,
To know full well what love itself does deem.
But we were in a dire circumstance.
Too quickly did Time part us as two friends.
A fatalist would blame it all on chance,
And some would say that friendship never ends.
Yet this I know, had we not been so young,
Not so much time would we have left to spend
To thus be parted, I without a tongue
More lines to Marlowe's salty poem to lend.
Had we been old, this parting would be brief,
Not sixty years or more and all that grief.

8

Should summer come again and you're not here,
Should trees put on their green and I'm alone,
Should flowers bloom in gardens when a tear
Falls in my heart which quickly turned to stone?
I think of all the happy days we had;
We ran through fields and looked for butterflies,
We sang each other songs, and we were glad,
We looked and saw each other in our eyes.
If I could see myself reflect in you,
And you could see yourself reflect in me,
Were we not friends and to each other true,
For then we had each other's eyes to see.
Yet, look into this tear that's grown pool-size;
It's your dear image, and that image cries.

9

When I do think upon that old man, Time,
And how through these quick years he's tortured me,
Destroying all that's rich and half sublime
By parting us across a wide dark sea;
When I do think what that old man has done,
Who swallowed up the hours of sweet days
And took away the apples of the sun
And covered up your face with veils of haze,
Then would I like to stab him with a knife
And gouge his eyes and pierce his heart straight through,
And disembowel and cut him to his life,
Till pale and spent, an offering to you.
A murder that I never will commit—
Yet send me Time, and never would I quit.

10

The clock still beats its iron hands around,
Foretelling minutes, hours, and the days;
The elm leaves drop and drift upon the ground;
Portending doom, Time sings an autumn phrase.
Then he with dull and ragged sickle edge
Does cut and lop the flowers from the fields;
A single bird flies chirping in the hedge,
Some broken notes but music never yields.
And I, Time's sop, obsequious a fool.
Do take my pen to write of you a word,
But in my hand I cannot wield this tool,
And what I write of you, Time makes absurd.
Yet if I cannot of you, dear friend, write,
I will not wind my foe, the clock, tonight.

11

Upon this stormy early autumn day
The rain comes falling down, and thunder roars;
The sun since early morn has gone away,
And lazy shadows sleep behind shut doors.
The first of fall is purring in the leaves,
The sunset rain, like blood it will appear,
The corn in fields is gathered into sheaves,
And from my room a chirping bird I hear.
A counterpoint to drops of falling rain,
The lightning strikes and lightens up the sky;
The sky will weep against my windowpane,
I think it is myself that I see cry.
For since you are away my tears, like rain,
Stain green leaves red, till you are back again.

12

It is the midst of autumn come at last,
Red leaves begin to fall like drops of blood,
The glories of the summer done and past,
And autumn rains come on us like a flood.
The pools of leaves now gather on the ground,
The reds and golds and pinks upon the breeze,
The goldenrods will fall without a sound,
And fruits no longer hang upon the trees.
But in my garden blooms a single rose,
As crimson as its petals is my blood,
And where there is a rose I know he goes—
Till those bright petals fall, a crashing thud.
For how can roses hold to stems and cling,
If I cannot of my dear young friend sing?

13

But let the leaves like drops of blood still fall,
And let the rose's petals wait and wilt,
And lie like corpses just outside my hall
The pools of leaves that soon will turn to silt.
For I have raised a castle in my mind,
And round the castle fortresses I've built
To keep away the corpses and the wind,
So autumn gales will not my castle tilt.
Now no dispute have I against Time's way;
Let breathy autumn come with pent-up rage
And strew my hall with leaves day after day,
And let a death the fallen leaves presage.
For I, locked up inside my castle tight,
All day of spring and you, sweet friend, will write.

14

It is that time again when I must write,
It is that time again when I must sing
To ward off evil dreams that come at night,
The monstrous images they tend to bring.
Last night I dreamed you sat beside a pool,
Mid-autumn, and the trees around all red,
And suddenly beside yourself a ghoul—
With open mouth, it flung me from my bed.
And witches flew across the slender moon,
And goblins whispered in the darkened glen.
"It cannot be, your death has come too soon—"
I know I gasped and stabbed them with my pen.
This morning, after dreaming hours and hours,
My bed is red with blood. mine, theirs, or yours?

15

The days grow short, the light too soon goes dim,
No flowers in my garden left to pluck,
No bright bouquets that I can pick for him,
No honeyed flowers for the bees to suck.
It is the autumn coming on of frost,
Bright yellow leaves all touch the ground and break.
Without him in my garden I am lost,
I do not sleep because I'd have to wake.
Without him I am like those same sad bees
That seek for sugared nectar that's not there;
For he is many miles across the seas,
A friend of mine who once stood here so fair.
And I am like a fallen fractured leaf,
Cold sun illuminates my heart of grief.

16

The sun is bright, and clear and blue the sky,
The yellow leaves hang trembling in trees,
Except for those that huddled under lie
In formless piles that shiver in the breeze.
Last night the frost lay on the final flowers,
All night with them did his cold fingers play.
As virgins that despoiled weep on for hours,
They wait the sun to wilt them all away.
Last night I heard a stirring in the glen
Some witches who upon old brooms do ride;
I dreamed I saw you with the witches then,
And I awoke and found that I had cried.
For witches steal a friend away from friend
And 'gainst them no one can a friend defend.

17

The virgin flowers make a sacrifice;
October frost, with him they are in league,
And when the moon is big with two dark eyes
They all the countryside with brooms besiege.
In Autumn they come flying from the North,
In hoards they fly across the first fall moon,
And then they send bewitcheries hence forth
And bring the killing winds that come too soon.
Dear friend, if with these witches now you lie,
Around your neck, I've placed an amulet.
Make all of them drop to the ground and die,
Touch thrice upon your head your green chaplet,
Then cross your hands across your trembling heart,
For only you can make the grim fiends part.

18

Today, while walking in the hidden glen,
The leaves upon the maple trees were red.
I found a broom upon the ground, and when
I looked around, I saw the witches dead.
They lay upon the leaves like rotting crows,
With yellow teeth and thick hair turned to grey;
They'll lie here now, I thought, until it snows,
And then by magic, they will fly away.
But for the time I know that you are free,
Still holds yet strong our friendship and our love.
Although you are not here to be with me,
My life will find the sunshine from above.
A heavy weight is lifted from my heart,
To know that fiends cannot two friends thus part.

19

My red geraniums are still in bloom;
The end of fall, and light goes dim too soon,
The golden elms put on their wintry gloom,
Yet still I sing to you like some buffoon.
The season of the sun is gone at last,
Another year, and you have been away.
The glad spring's beauty faded all too fast,
Yet still I have a thousand things to say.
If time and space could loosen ties with earth
And we were free to meet when we did want,
Then every day my face would be all mirth
And you the sun that now takes on a slant.
The flowers then would yield to winter's blast,
Yet snow will hold our friendship safe and vast.

20

And I a leaf that trembles on the bough
In autumn once the early frost is past;
I am a leaf who mighty Time does cow,
But I beseech Him, let me one day last!
In earnest I implore to Time, my foe,
To let me stay for but the briefest day;
Obsequiously I tell him that I'll go,
Then do I wait for what he has to say.
For like a leaf I'm covered o'er with dust,
The dust of Time that makes my eyes go dim;
For like a leaf, upon my blade is rust,
I, sycophant, must duly bow to him.
And I will do whatever old Time bids,
Till you return to brush him off my lids.

21

For every leaf that falls, a scream I hear,
The oaks and maples all seem drenched in blood;
And every leaf that falls is but a tear
That falls on forest ground to make a flood.
Or try to say that it is otherwise,
That only leaves are falling from the trees,
Then have the trees put on some cruel disguise,
Some victim in the woods to scare and seize?
The thirsty murderer is in the woods,
The slasher with his knife, that will turn red;
I've seen him walk at day, all wrapped in hoods,
And slash the trees to make the leaves fall dead.
The cold of pain, of falling from a tree,
Is like myself when you're not here with me.

22

The trees have known of my sad lonely grief,
The flowers shed their limpid weeping tears;
Now on the trees there's not a single leaf,
And frost has crusted flowers onto biers.
'Tis late October, and the leaves are down,
An early snow has fallen to the ground.
The sun behind the clouds, bedraggled clown,
Has finished out another annual round.
The seasons come, the seasons come and go,
And now you are not with me, my dear friend,
From joyous summer into winter snow,
All things must cease, all things must have their end.
And though the trees and flowers wept for me,
Through my own frozen tears I cannot see.

23

I know full well that winter lies ahead,
And that the trees have lost their golden leaves,
And that chrysanthemums have all gone dead.
A swan upon the lake alone, she grieves.
I know full well that the glad summer's past,
And all the leaves have fallen in a heap,
And this warm day will not much longer last,
The low sad sun too early goes to sleep.
Still in transition, summer day to fall,
This lull in grim Time's ever-quickening pace
I hear that lone swan to her mate give call,
I will the trees with thoughts of you enlace.
And thus while you are gone, on this brief day
Some lacy leaves still hang to trees and stay.

24

Knowing how many other poets wrote
Of this same theme of friendship cut in two,
Sometimes I hesitate to strike a note,
Yet still I know they did not write of you.
And you, dear friend, deserve a poet's grace,
And friendship strong should never ever die;
When I recall a smile upon your face,
I call you angel, and I do not lie.
A laurel friendship ours so rich deserves,
For never were two friends more true than we.
No matter what the harshest fate us serves,
I am compelled to write of you and me.
So still of you, my friend, I will indite,
O most dear friend, of whom I'll always write.

25

Like perfumed petals of an autumn rose,
Or sometimes strong as lilacs when they bloom,
Your image comes and lingers and it goes,
Then leaves me far behind to face a gloom.
Sometimes so dark and lonely and so deep,
I would your image then would never come;
For then for nights and nights I cannot sleep
But must count sheep and never find the sum.
And if I never could your love regain,
I do not think that I should want to live;
What brings me joy must also bring me pain—
For all the pain, it too a joy does give.
And that's a thought by which I have to learn,
That but through pain can I such sweet joy earn.

26

If lines of poetry I could indite,
Then every one I would express to you;
For now you are no longer in my sight,
A bright quickness has lost its brightest hue.
Although to others you appeared a man,
To me you always were a unicorn,
A legendary beast that danced and ran,
With laughing sides and smooth and golden horn.
I'd write of maidens and a sacrifice,
Of how an old man shot a unicorn
Whom all the maidens wished they could entice,
Of how it died and how its flesh was torn.
But oh, dear friend, because I cannot write,
I'll go in search of unicorns tonight.

27

If we should meet again after the years
Have quite worn out themselves to dust and clay,
Then I would need to stifle all my fears
That I would find our friendship did not stay.
For I would stand and tremble like the moon,
Afraid to see a frown to cloud my face,
Afraid to see a false smile come too soon—
And would we stand apart or quick embrace?
For I have known on meeting other friends
Huge gaps of time can find their way between;
I've seen how friendship dear, it simply ends
As though the friends had never ever been.
But this I pray will ever be our lot
That our dear friendship will not be forgot.

28

Should twenty years have come and gone, still yet
Like Troilus for you I'd gladly wait,
And there beside the garden's wall I'd fret
And view each passer pass my garden gate.
Should forty years too quickly pass me by,
I still would pick the blooms of summer flowers,
Like lonely Troilus I'd wait and sigh,
While Time made minutes sad unfold to hours.
Should sixty summers turn my hair to grey,
Still in my garden would I always be,
To wait dear friend for you, "Hello" to say,
To wait alone for you again to see.
Let Time advance and do whate'er he will,
Like Troilus, I will wait your coming still.

29

Like tombstones the November trees are cold,
And all my griefs are buried under them;
So many more than e're my heart could hold,
My hand is also like a withered limb.
I cannot say our love has lost its leaves,
And yet it seems that barren does it stand
Like naked trees upon which cold ground heaves
With winter frost, and I without a wand
To call some magic spring to our sweet love,
Again to make our cherry garden bloom.
The emptiness upon the ground above
Portends our fate and our predestined doom.
But this I know, love always goes with grief,
And I must hope this winter to be brief.

30

Still while the quiet snow will come and fall
There is a thought that grips with sudden fears,
What if to someone else your heart will call,
What if your heart my heart no longer hears?
Will winter winds convert our love to ice,
Will winter storms with rude and cold hands grope
Beneath the snow to find wherefore love lies,
Erupt, erode the coming on of hope?
Must all our love be but a memory,
A fallen frozen bird beneath the snow?
These are but some of all the things I see,
That love detached again can never grow.
Yet when grim evenings creep across the skies,
My heart still leaps from frozen boughs and flies.

31

I sense the yearly coming on of spring,
A merriment becomes the earth's refrain.
I fly about the woods with broken wing
And almost hope the winter would remain.
My songs I sang to you, though they still rhyme,
They caw about my head like rasping crows,
The jingles jangled out of step and time;
And if I cannot sing, my heart well knows
The image of our love will fade away
As quick as snow from off the meadow fields.
And how should we each to the other stay
If I can't write a song to love that yields
Forever in my heart your image true,
But bleat among the fields, a lambless ewe?

32

The ice again has melted from the lakes,
The elms along my street are all in bloom,
The robin in my garden early wakes,
And yet this spring does come with certain gloom.
The sun shines bright as ever on the hills,
I turn to them, to springtime's brightest green,
My garden's smallest stream, it gently fills
From melting snow, but still I have not seen
Your face among the flowers on the rocks
Where I did see your image long ago;
Some beast inside my mind your picture blocks,
And I must sit beside my stream in woe.
But this my solid promise on this day,
That beast on you, my friend, will never prey.

33

Last night too long in threat'ning dreams I slept,
A hoard of fiendish beasts and dragons tossed
Upon the shores of my dim mind and crept
One beast into my inner eye, sight lost.
It was the beast that made your image blocked
From memory when days before I sat
Inside myself and found your face out-locked,
A gruesome beast, all red and scales and fat.
Inside myself, inside my garden wall,
The beast consumed nigh every leaf and tree;
I thought I heard you from the garden call,
When I awoke, you were not there with me.
A beast did creep inside me and there slept;
If I did catch a glimpse of you, you wept.

34

Come fiend, come dragon, come all-hellish beast,
You will not with my dear friend's image flee;
For I will let my words upon you feast,
And you'll contend with swords, and words, and me.
A golden circle placed upon your head,
A magic circle round you I will weave,
Transform to silver hooves now made of lead,
And then, brute beast, from garden's path you'll leave
And with my sword I will now make you bleed,
Your blood will fall like petals from a rose,
Into my heart a newly nurtured seed
Until his picture new spring plants enclose,
Until you're forced into to your deathly grace
And, drowned in seas of nightmare, find your place.

35

The beast that crept into my bed and slept,
I've managed now to banish from the rose,
And though, dear friend, I know how much you've wept,
You stand with flowers in majestic pose.
Again has come another lovely spring,
The birds are singing in the budding tree,
And you, dear friend, are found in everything,
Though still between us lies the endless sea.
I see your face in every flower I meet,
Your image seems to cling upon the air,
With fresh smiles you and I each other greet,
And all the sky is calm and blue and fair.
So long as pictures from these words can flow,
Then every seed I plant, I know will grow.

36

Accept of me these penciled-out bouquets,
That grew inside the garden of my heart,
And read each word until that word portrays
Our friendship and the music that will start
And play among the images of poem;
With lyre and lute, play the music swift
Until you find yourself again at home,
Until you find my garden is your loft.
Bring choir boys to harmonize each note,
And let us under trees in memory lie,
And look for other flowers that I wrote,
And breathe their scent before they wilt and die.
For then, my friend, to me you would return
And never for you would I need to yearn.

37

Around the clock the hands still pulse and move,
And still, dear friend, you are not with me here
I wait and think that you I must reprove,
But there is too much something of a fear.
For what if you, dear friend, should not return,
Or what if, on your journey, you are lost?
And what if armies your abode do burn,
And what if seas a fragile ship has tossed?
The days, the weeks, the months, the years go by;
I turn the pages of my calendar.
Each time I turn another page, I sigh
And wonder just how long I can endure.
But this I know: forever will I wait
Till Time his ancient throne does abdicate.

38

I do not know, but why am I so sad?
The melancholies all about me hang.
Tho' from the birds the music should be glad,
'Tis solemn as what yesterday they sang.
The sadness hangs above me like a cloud,
Although the sun shines warm and bright today;
And melancholy wraps me like a shroud,
And on the strings of her sad harp does play.
The sky is blue, inside my heart falls rain
Which drops and drops in flowers hidden there
Which seem to hang their heads as if in pain,
And in my heart droop flowers everywhere.
So no relief to suffering they bring,
Not here and now nor ever will you sing.

39

The letter came, the letter came today,
With sad, sad news that told me you were dead.
I could not make the letter go away.
Your father wrote, "My son, my son is dead.
My son was killed upon the battlefield,
Two raging countries took away my son,
The ancient foes, their deadly banners yield
My sweetest fruit, and what is done is done.
My son, your friend, lies sleeping in the ground;
His mother, brother, sister, and I weep
For what is left of him, a little mound,
Where I a silent, restless vigil keep.
My dear sweet son lies buried in the ground,
And from his lips I cannot hear a sound."

40

Your father lost a son, I lost a friend.
In losing you there is a double woe;
Oh, how could I suspect such tragic end?
And yet the letter came and said 'tis so.
A double woe? Ten thousand double woes.
Your wound has turned my garden stream to red;
Oh, why must war exist between two foes,
When war makes sons and friends and lovers dead?
My garden mocks me with a bloody stream,
The petals on the rose are drops of blood;
Again I read the letter and I scream.
I feel my burning eyes go moist and flood.
Upon the letter fall, drop after drop,
The tears of blood that seem to never stop.

41

What lovely Nature made so kind, grim Death
Did take away and leave a sudden hush;
For from his lips, half-parted, came no breath,
Upon his cheek no slightest hint of blush.
What lovely Nature showed, did that Death grim
Strike down in one quick swoop upon the field;
And like a flower struck by frost, on him
Did Death his ugly, swollen, hard sword wield.
What lovely Nature gave, that grim Death took,
Unto the boy a filthy deed, unkind,
And even crept into his grave and hid
To sleep with him who left me all behind.
But I, dear friend, will Death's foul deed undo
By writing lines of poems, or die with you.

42

The oceans seems so many miles across.
One time I thought again to see your face,
But now I sit accounting my great loss,
Or walk about my room, or stand, or pace.
The rain keeps falling from the sullen skies,
It seems for months and years I've been morose.
Outside within my rain-drenched garden lies
Upon the ground a single fallen rose.
Some petals there lie scattered on the ground.
In rain some flowers never come to bloom,
But all their petals scattered lie around,
Bright colors augment dark and awful gloom.
Your death, Ali, did come but all too soon!
Could these dark skies again reveal the moon?

43

Has come again to bless the gardens 'round
The time of year of apple-blossom air.
Scattered petals wilt upon the ground,
But for the most, the air is sweet and fair.
And trees now sing with beautiful bright birds,
Where branches once were leafless, dull, and bare;
They almost seem to sing with soothing words,
To paint the landscape budding everywhere.
The woods are pink and lavender with flowers,
With lilacs wild and iris days unfold
It seems they dare to bloom for endless hours,
And only later will their truth be told.
But apples in my orchards do not bloom,
It seems your death has brought to them their doom.

44

And so must I begin to plow and till
A magic garden in the fields of mind.
With images, I will my garden fill
And under some bright tree your picture find.
No cold from years ago but flesh and blood,
Your arms, your face, your hands I'll see again,
For images are only made of wood,
But I choose flesh with blood and joy with pain.
The tree will be the brightest carat gold,
Yet breathe with leaves upon the gentle wind,
And I to you will rush with arms to hold,
And kiss your cheek, and know I've never sinned.
For artists' minds can do what minds can do,
Forever make our friendship to renew.

45

And in the magic garden of my mind,
Again, Ali, will you and I find grace,
And from that death your face will be unlined,
Returned to youth your sweet, kind smiling face.
Again we'll through the lovely meadows walk
And watch for butterflies that rest and flit,
Again will we delight to laugh and talk,
And near some quiet, peaceful stream we'll sit.
For Time can't touch inside my garden wall,
And Death can't take a friend away from friend.
We'll to each other hear each other call,
The golden tree to death will never bend.
My words to you, Ali, are almost lined,
And in these words I hope yourself to find.

46

With simple words I think that death I've slain,
Rude-fingered Time, it seems, had never been,
Though they with you, Ali, for years have lain,
I look around my mind, and they're not seen.
If I have chosen other poets' rhymes,
If I have chosen other poets' verse,
The poet friends of mine in other times,
It is because I did their lines rehearse.
Like Chaucer, Spenser, Milton, Donne, and Will
These poets taught me one important thing,
The artist's mind can drive away all fear
Of time and death because the tongue can sing.
And death and time I think I have undone,
And now I see the coming on of sun.

Metamorphoses

When sudden showers lifted scents of lilac, plum, and rose along the trails, 'twas old sorceress Mearth coming her rueful way again. Warmed by her south spring winds, Dane, the knight who in orchard slept, awakened to the flowering fields and trees, forgetting his icy dreams of winter eves. Under a gay sky wet with mirth, he drank the distillation of her rain and was blinded by her flowery breath. And thus arrived the doom that wears a fairy's face, creeping like worms upon these vernal hours. Donning his helmet, which had lain all winter beneath the silent moon, Dane looked to the woods beyond the orchard bowers. And he started up that gnarled winding trail. As the narrow path began to wane, he heard the water pounding on rocks. Clutching the moss-grown towers rising from the water's edge, he grieved for a lovely maid therein.

For days and months, the maid, quick-spinning at her wheel, had watched for the knight, hoping he might pass along below the crag. And as his red plume came into view, her fretting turned to a smile. With silken threads wrapped round her ankle, she waved and called to him, "O knight, it's not yet noon." He could not make out the guile upon her face, but like the eye will catch a glint of steel, his eye caught her waving speck of rag, and her voice sent strumming song upon his heart. What knight whose heart so strummed can help but feel like a stallion or a stag? More so felt Dane, his head still numb with tangled dreams of winter gloom, love's nectar on his lips long dried. So quickly did he raise his hand and kneel, then crawled and leapt over sharp rocks and broken slag. Stumbling, trying to run but instead slipping on the

79

weeds that clung to the rocks. And finally he fell and struck his head.

The Maiden, lynx-eyed, looked on him bound in the iron jaws of seaweeds heaped upon the rocks. Then swiftly she changed from maid to a monstrous crow, perched upon her window ledge. With threads still wrapped around her claws, she beat her thund'rous wings and down to the rocks she flew. Swooping low, she wove her threads around the knight. Like a spider, she spun her silken threads around the victim in her web. The knight, now helpless as hart or roe, in her clutches once more fell to sleep. She dragged her warm prey to the cliff's sharp edge, then flew to return to her tower.

Bringing a torch which spit and spattered on her knight, she pulled the threads to see that they were solid. With a cackle, she mended where they'd rubbed against his sword. And shaking and twitching, she drove a stake into Dane's heart, and collected his blood in a jade cup into which she sprinkled a powder black. The purple rank liquid she poured upon the knight and uttered dark words, "In forest glade, as in a wild wood Crisseyde was boared, so you as hog will maiden tear to shreds."

As Circe drove her herd of savage hogs, so this maid drove Dane down the stair—across the rocks, around the bay, along the seashore strung with shells—until she brought him to a leafy wood. Pools filled with frogs, strange birds singing, a hare hopping in the clover, and many beasts and men cast under spells—each wearing near his heart a mark of blood. She pulled her knight-turned-boar over moss-grown logs, rotten stumps, and foul mushrooms. In streams thick with clay, the maiden laughing drove him on. Flogging her bristled boar, she drove him to a hidden den where oft she came to play nine years ago before she heard the bells and ran to see the fairies. Thinking on them, the maiden could still feel the toads crawling in her hair when she was turned to witch. For this she drives her knight, to free herself from witchenhood.

For this she turned the knight into a boar. Noon-day sport for Mearth,

80

black sorceress who held between her breasts the rotten summer rose. With blackest law, the fairies rent the heart of every maid that passed their boggy heather trails. One night they caught Lucia on the moor, and her ghost still flits over moonlit pool. Maria's hair is wound in a raven's nest. This spring the bog lake flooded with maiden woes. On lonesome heath the fairies caught Lenore. They strung her hair with toads and worms and left her on a floor of bright leaves where, try as she may, she could not free herself from the horrors.

So Lenore turned mad and laughed when she would weep. But screamed she did when upon her the lanky boar did leap. And so old Mearth performed her wicked rite. And as soon as that foul act on maid was done, the boar returned to knight. On his bright mail the threads of maiden spun. He saw the boar tracks and the blood hanging like dew on tree and rock and fern. He saw the maiden there undone, a faded rose upon her leafy bed. He saw how she'd wept and bled, her wrists still wound with silken threads. Away from her he turned.

As soon as the spell was lifted, fairies swarmed into the bloody den. With fairy swords they beat and stung the knight, who burdened by guilt could not find the strength to flee. With roots and vines of trailing grape, they slashed and bound the knight. Who knows what Mearth will do when she goes mad? Through horrid winter dreams, she made those fairies bad if ever they were good. And Dane to them a sport.

And when they finished sporting, the fairies hastened to the maid forlorn. They gathered up the heap of maid and rags and carried her through gloomy trees mossy winding ways, where at times a lamenting ghost appears, playing pipes of bones. Then down to rocky jags, they wound their way to a wooded lake. Upon its wet brim, trilling with mourning birds, they placed Lenore within a boat that blew from leeward shore.

Sweet Lenore sleeping still drifted across the lake. She dreamed that from her window she espied a red-plumed gallant knight. He looked into her maiden eyes. And her eyes to him held fast as if to sun. Yet how far adrift from that fair dream she lay!

When old Mearth saw the boar destroy the maid, such lively sport she thought she'd never seen. Sorceress in cobweb gown gleamed upon the scene and felt her passions rise. So many knights and maidens here will drown, wrapped in her vernal arms of freshest green. What could Mearth care the fairies brought a crown to make the maiden Lenore their new queen? For seven days, this maid lay in a trance and drifted on the lake to fairyland, when at last the boat was landed on a gated shoal, guarded by a stony troll. The fairies bowed and knelt, and then the gate unlocked and the fairies entered in. They sang and danced around Lenore, who woke upon this fair expanse of castles built on purple sand, of winding paths and flowery boughs and orchards ripe with fruit.

Still in that fairyland the maiden rules. Sometimes she thinks she sees some laughing ghouls who feed upon a knight. And she wakes herself from dreams that make her crawl and feel ablaze. The maid Lenore, who was once fair and chaste, sees a shadow riding up the wall. A knight comes riding from thick-walled haze. Sometimes the maiden walks by moonlit pools. She sees upon the pools her maiden waste, as thick as autumn leaves that on her fall. Come quickly, autumn leaves, in these sad days. Let oak and maple send the sugar to their roots, for once again to set the world to sleep.

Ode to the Seasons

I

The green and glad of spring have come again,
The trees are filled with sweet melodious air
Of birds that sing between the drops of rain,
While apple trees are filled with sweet buds fair.
Once more the robin on the lawn is seen,
Once more the woods with flowers all are dressed,
Once more the meadow lark does sing his song
Among the pink and green;
And now it sees that all the world is blessed,
As lovely Venus does the days prolong.

Glad Venus has her mantle all unfurled,
And every glade is green with sanctity;
Fresh music seems to dance throughout the world,
The woods, the town, and city sing to me.
With beauty pregnant now is mother earth,
All seems it is a pleasant laughing dream,
Like robin eggs, light blue within the nest,
It is a glorious birth;
At evening time I sit beside a stream
And watch the sun behind the trees take rest.

Next day again the brightest sun comes round,
And all the birds are waking in the trees,
Fresh meadows with fresh flowers all abound,
And I am glad to see what my eye sees.
It's sanctity my heart desires to give
To Venus with her lovely mantle spread.
The flowers bring us back to sanity,
All creatures want to live;
I feel a music hang about my head,
"Tis spring 'tis spring, and all is gaiety.

II

With Dionysus summer makes its fuss,
The blush of spring has turned to darkest greens,
And all your nymphs do say, "Come dance with us,"
The peacock in the garden struts and preens.
By brooks and streams I've seen the bracken fern,
I've tasted juicy berries in the wood,
At evening time I've seen the fireflies
Ignite their lights and burn.
And under silvery moon I've often stood
And heard the fleet, fleet nighthawk's screaming cries.

The sun shines bright and happy all the day,
And roses everywhere are full in bloom,
The children run upon the shore and play,
There is no thunderstorm portending gloom.
It is the brightest day in mid-July,
The pure blue lake is placid ever yet,
Reflecting all the bluest sky above,
The bluest, bluest sky.
Oh come bright sun and never ever set,
Let Dionysus feed us with her love.

Let Dionysus bring about the wine,
'Tis time to eat, to drink, and merry be;
And let the tender grape the oak entwine,
Oh, brightest summer sunshine, stay with me!
If not forever, stay then for awhile,
And let us all again young children be,
Or let young lovers never ever part,
And let's the time beguile;
Forever will we be all summer free,
The summer sun shall ever fill my heart.

III

But summer sun has lost its brightest smile,
Now Neptune sports upon the sylvan shore,
To paint the leaves with fire for awhile,
The evenings growing chill, unlike before.
The meadow lark again has ceased its song,
The robins gather, flying to the south,
The partridge circles back into its nest.
The days are not so long.
And Neptune blows the water from his mouth,
His colder gales are now upon us loosed.

The farmer starts to gather all his grain,
The fields are cut, and hay in piles lies.
This season comes not to me without pain,
Forlorn, a lover sits in woods and sighs.
But now it's time to gather second oats,
For now it's time of harvest come around,
And now it's time to take what good earth yields.
The lakes are without boats.
The fruits in gardens now do they abound,
Fall flowers still are blooming in the fields.

But for a little while will they yet bloom,
And then they will be cut by Neptune's frost,
The sky will overcast with deadly gloom,
And they to Neptune's winds will all be lost.
The maple leaves have turned to yellow-red,
The willow by the brook has lost her leaves,
The oak prepares to dress himself in brown,
And all the birds have fled.
A lover sits within the woods and grieves,
The sky puts on its late autumnal frown.

IV

The harshest season, winter, has come round,
Now Saturn has his day and so must time,
While all the leaves have fallen to the ground,
And all my pain, bare branches seem to mime.
For spring, summer, and autumn are but brief,
And I could hold them, all three, in my hand,
With tulips, roses, asters, one bouquet
To hide a lover's grief.
Alone by frozen lake I sometimes stand
And know that winter's snow is here to stay.

Most sad and cruelest season of the year
When all the plants have withered from the lake
The yellow willow dares not shed a tear,
Because the tear would fall on ice and break.
The winter winds from Saturn's lips are chill,
The days are grey and cold and white and bleak,
And everywhere I look I see the snow;
And Venus on her hill,
Enshrouded, for Adonis does she seek,
And all around the winter winds do blow.

Untimely Time, old Saturn's only child,
Why must you come, why must you stay so long?
You are an aged child that haunts the wild;
Although a child, yet you are mighty strong.
But you are given an immortal youth,
Forever growing old then young again,
And even in this winter's frozen snow
There lies a secret truth:
That Venus shall no longer stay in pain,
When Saturn to her makes his sign below.

Iran

FROM A PERSIAN SONG

—A translation

I want to see you
In the darkness of the night.
I want to see you and your hands
In the silent hush of sleeping.

I will gather all the butterflies of our house,
And with colored pencils
I will write your name
On their wings.

I will not sleep at night;
I will fly like a swallow
And go near the stars.
I will knot them in the corner of my shirt,
And tomorrow I will hang them in your hands.

I will wear your shoes;
Perhaps I will be with you now
Returned for a moment.
You will see that I am running.

RAMADAN

Green algae gathers in pools.
Frogs float in tepid water.
A black scorpion dances,
Glints across my desert path,
And looks at me from the top of his eyes.

I am left alone with the moon
And the memory of white daisies
Growing among rocks in mountain streams.

Tomorrow the monotony of a sultry sky goes on forever
And the mourning of people dressed in black.
Blood is spread at the doorway of each house,
And the echo of a bleating lamb
Hangs as sharp as a knife in the air,
And as heavy as sorrow.

My brain feels numb with a pain
Like the sting of a scorpion,
Like a scream that can't get out.

I gaze from my windows for hours,
And in the midst of unending wailing
Dream steadily towards flowers
Growing among rocks in mountain streams.

IRAN, 1985

From desert fields where soldiers die alone
The children of the rising dawn come home.
All night two sides were locked in mortal war,
Two warring sides in battles thick with blood.
All night the heavy boom of canons heard,
The weeping and the sighs of those dear men.
What young child could holy Persian priest
Cajole, deceive, to give his life for him?
But see that they, a mere eleven years,
Or younger, running down to barely eight,
Return to village greens, what's left of them.
This country's king, his scepter must throw down,
Alas, an old priest picked it up again.
But who could pique the conscience of a king,
Or salve resentment in an hostile priest?
And in a common grave their children lay.
But wars are all decreed by older men
Who send young men to war to fight for them;
Tell me, what death should be more rich than life?

What sacrifice can justify the pain
Of a sad child who knows he breathes his last,
Not even strength enough to brush the tears,
The terrible silence that precedes each death?

This sacrifice so grand to eulogize:
I have seen fear in many young men's eyes.
How strict their diplomacy might have been
If wars were only fought between old men.
Philosophize from pulpit, chair, and throne—
Glory to dying brave young men or them?
Say children eight, eleven, or eighteen—

What right has president, or priest, or king
To pad his pride with them, the young victims?
And all the wars that have been fought for pride!
Surely there must come the day, the light
When that to live these children have first right.

Women Across the Ages

LIDO

The queenly sea nymphs and maidens,
Unfolding their wings on the shore,
Like roses laden with moonlight
Or ferns on the new forest floor.

Or like moths new flown in summer,
They flutter and laugh with their wings;
And the sea wind heavy with moonlight
Through shells on the shore hums and sings.

The sea is a garden of moons,
Like roses we drift on the sea,
The sea undulating and singing
Under nymphs and maidens and me.

All night we drift on the sea foam,
We bloom and we burst and we drown;
And the wings of the nymphs and the maidens
To the dark sea floor flutter down.

Today, our sea-blown bodies
Are empty shells tossed on the sand;
Our hearts ripped out by the sea waves,
Our mouths cast up on the strand.

The shells and bones from the sea floor
Dry pallid and pink where they're flung;
And here yet wet with the sea foam
A sea-torn weed has been flung.

The pearly eyes of dead sleepers
Are tossed from their shells on a stone;
The sea foam pops on the pebbles,

The petals of roses are strewn.

The low moon, bloody with roses,
Sinks, weeping the queens from their thrones;
This evening a wreath of roses
Is flung where I gather their bones.

ARACHNIA

My love, beneath this tree today
I see inside your eyes the leaves
Of autumn trees above your head,
The hidden bones of bodies far away.

Like mushrooms stemming out of earth
Under the lacy fronds of ferns,
The bones lie quiet in the leaves
Transuding to their mossy birth.

Where they still lie among the leaves,
White splintered bones mossed over green,
A spider drops inside their eyes,
Flings his net, and weaves and weaves.

Not from the fall of someone's tears
They kiss, with bony mouths still wet
From moss and grass and leaves or sweat
Of lust-fire riding on their fears.

Inside the hollow of their eyes
The moon is weeping golden tears;
Inside the echo of their sighs
The spider spins and waits for flies.

My blood is filled with passion-milk;
Your deep-pool eyes are golden brown;
But what is this across your brow?
Your silky hair, or spider silk?

LILITH

Sipping wine, she plays the lute
Keeping inside her golden cage.
Her hazel eyes, her lips are mute.
The evening sleeps beside the mountains,
The water falls deep in the fountains;
She spins herself into the strings,
She spins a net around my wings,
She does not see this swelling rage.
Sipping again the wine, she weaves,
Nor sees my fingers at her cage.
I do not know what stops the motion
Of two people slept to love—
How it becomes a dead emotion.
Waking in the morn, we see
The petals fallen from the tree
And hear the rain fall on the leaves
And silent lute-strings stilled.

MILTON'S DAUGHTER

I see the pen is on the table
And the paper to write on;
I cannot see the muse's words.
Who only stands and stands and waits.

Dear Daughter, I now tell thee—
For I am blind—to write the words
Just as the muse tells them to me;
Write down the words and say them back.

Dear Father, where did Adam go?
You may well ask, dear Daughter mine:
Where did Adam and his Eve go
Across the fields, the Garden closed?

Daughter dear, think of this:
Adam must stand alone and wait,
Until his dear Eve comes along,
Wait for her at the Garden gate.

I do not know where they did flee
Beneath a bank of flowers true
The land is closed to my closed eyes—
But dear Daughter, I still have you.

CELIA

Tonight you wear your hair
Upon your skull, still golden,
Glowing softly in the wind
Among the mosses and the springs
Small lily flowers.

Your eyes are empty mirrors
Of moonlight eyes remembered
Under lilacs and the moon
A year ago, when you picked
Lilies for your hair.

Tonight I hear within
The hollow of your ears
The echo of the night bird song
Lost upon the leaves
Here where the moon shines
Silver in the pools
Like ghosts that walked
Among your childhood fears.

Lady of sorrow,
If I could spin to life
Again your flesh, my love
I'd spin till kingdom come.

LUCY

Tonight we still wear roses in our hair
Even though the drops of blood will stain
Our cheeks where yesterday were tears:

Let us go near the quiet river
When the moon swims among the trees,
Let us walk softly over
The silver drops of dew.

Do not disturb these silent waters,
For the moon and web might break
And, O my love, if the moon should pass,
And these webbed jewels in the grass

Should crash on this new evening
When we wear roses in our hair,
My heart could not remake itself again.

LUCY BROWN

Nor willow, elm, nor oak can stop their tears;
See how the leaves collect in shallow pools;
It's late October, and the grave is dug;
To Lucy's lover the mourners bid adieu.

One by one the leaves come whispering down,
Together gather on this silent hill;
Upon the grave a wreath of roses lies,
Red for the passion left in Lucy's heart.

The mourners all retreat into their homes,
And Lucy stands beside the grave alone;
Like tombstones the tall naked trees appear,
As last leaves fall and float in Lucy's tears.

The leafless tress and Lucy Brown will weep,
Their tears like crystal ice hang in the wind,
Their tears so cold the sun cannot them melt,
And Lucy's heart a bird against the thorns.

Soon snow will drift across her lover's grave,
And Lucy'll wrap herself in a black shawl,
Hold in her hands a mirror and a comb,
Like Venus waiting for Adonis still.

ANNIE

Seeking to find the echo
But lost her voice
Fading with the now dimly lit skies
After the rains have washed out
The rainbows and flowers from my eyes.

Again sand washes into pebbles
Of shadows on the shore
Things change after the rains
The eyes are lost
And the silence is loud.

Shall the sparrows
Sing sweetly to the dawn
Above dust and ashes
When the wind discovers
The trees again.

And I can only reply
The beauty of the trees
The lunar moth footprints
In the sands we've trod
A new Moon coming from the Sun.

TO VENUS

There never was a mistress wanted more
From me than you demand, mother of love,
Especially now that spring comes marching in,
And flowers in my garden start to grow.

I love the birds and roses on your gown;
A Botticelli couldn't have painted more;
And, though I'm not Adonis, I have known
The first faint blush of pink upon your hand.

Venus, lovely Venus, goddess of love,
Prick me just so that I might feel no pain,
Or little pain, that I might feel you more,
For surely I account loving no sin.

Queen of spring, let April flowers in,
Let Time once more into an infant turn,
And let the winter that brought so much grief
Be banished that the leaf may put forth leaf.

Dedications

ELEGY FOR E.E.

—February 2011

In just spring time

When I get out old poems

    and i

read e.e. cummings' balloon man

    and i
think of You and your new hat

    and i

touch eternal youth and beauty

    and i
hear my heart

        sing
or

            weep

and indeed

      i do not

      know

MY FATHER'S EYES

—For Dr. Stockman

My father had such lovely eyes:
Eyes that looked for miles and miles
Beyond valleys, lakes, and fields
Through darkness of the church and trees
To city steps and rock-built walls;
Edifices not so tall which shade
At tables the crowded picnickers,
And in the sun the happy revelers
And now, although he's dead, they seem
To me a limitless demesne.

DEPARTURE

—For Dr. Stockman, December 2013

I shall remember upon your departure
Trees in blossom
Earth an efflorescence of color
And spring with its pristine blades of grass.
Suddenly the purple lilacs bloom,
A lavender coup of Whitman and Lincoln.

I shall remember your hair grown
Gray and thin as ashes,
The triumph of Time.

I shall remember swallows
Flying into blue sky—lapis lazuli of bird and feather
In pursuit of an eagle—Cyclopean eye
Plummeting toward earth and their home
To resume their brood.

Other Feelings

EPILOGUE

And Narcissus stood
Before the wild boar:
A primeval animal
From ancient times,
A primeval cannibal
Of the souls of men.
In all these old devourings
He ran against the sight of beauty
Because his eyes could not perceive
That beauty in the Soul conceives:
                    Desire: Love
And must have the flower,
Must have the fire.
Out of the wood the boar came,
And the young man stood before him.
Its tusk outstretching,
Its eyes cold as ice,
The boar roared and charged.
And Narcissus thought:
Perhaps the people cannot love
But someday they will
And I will kill this mad boar.
And he stood like a matador before a bull,
And struck, and the boar went down;
But it rose and with a tusk upturned
Caught the helpless man.

Like an eagle poised for flight,
Eyes uplifted to the sun,
And silent prayer fell to the earth,
And the boar darted aside and fell
And groaned and it too died.
Blood flowed freely from the man,

Ripped and strewn, like petals from a rose.
The clouds began to uncover the sun,
And the sky, and under it the tree,
The old tree weeping
Its purple petals down
To cover the bodies in the sand.
And the petals strewn
Began to drift in the wind
To the side waters of the ocean river,
And the blood seeped into the earth
And stained the mighty waters,
And the waves began to touch the shore,
Tenderly caressing the wound of the Earth.

The sun grew brighter;
The clouds went away;
And some small flame
Went up the waves
To the warm soothing light,
And his eyes closed out the sun,

And Narcissus lost sight
Of the other happenings of the day
And days and months and years to come.
Forever blooming, a golden flower
Blooms under the priest tree to the sun,
The flower of love,
Echoing love to the people.

HUBRIS

Throw him upon the rocks
Like the eagle, its talon clutched,
Throws the lion upon the rocks.
Man flies now in his flight to the sun.
Why would he fear that the rocks should catch him
Or break Him? But
He shall break; the earth cannot make a choice.
Up he climbs, one man against the purple sky
Till Icarus down the sky he comes—
And when it's done
Who has won?
The lion or the eagle,
Or the gulls that descend
To feed among the rocks?

TERRAINIA

She read poetry on the table
        amidst the corn and mosses;
        I took her down the paths
That went in and out in green leaves
        swaying up and down
        to the cornfields reading poetry;
On the table she stood clearly defined
        out of the grasses like Eve, on down
        the road among the corn
Or Ruth weeping ...

IMPOTENCE

A peculiar instinct, succinct
In time, wrecks the brain,
Grows dim.
Light sinks in around
      The pulled-down shades
Defining the darkness of the room
Arms outstretched, hopelessly
            reaching.
Mute. The silence is deep
      but no deeper than today
With all the noise of people.
Words uttered without contact
      but responded to
Destroy them.
Say nothing.
Arms outstretched. The tongue
        drawn back
Defining the darkness of the arms
      outstretched, hopelessly
          reaching
Tongue outstretched. The arms
        drawn back
Defining the vagueness of the tongue
        not speaking …

AT THE END OF A LONG SUMMER

Today, the eyes see,
The tongue bleeds,
The bodies disappear.
Snow buries the ground.
The corn stands parched
In the furrowed fields.
The snow falls fast on brooding blades,
The fingers stick in icy glades.
Today the sun blows, blinding me.

In the open field of dawn, yesterday
I saw with the sun the swaying and swinging
Of blooming bountiful bodies,
Of flesh firm and free.
I heard the green leaves
In the soft night wind
And the whispering sudden moon,
Now drying slowly and still in the night
Without the light of the distant star
Away today too far to see.

I hear the rattle and rustle in my ears
Of brown leaves scraping the walls,
Breaking to pieces inside, twitching.
Today the tongue is dry
And stumbles in the mouth.
The blades and bodies are furrowed under
The dust-filled eyes
Are heavy with the earth
Today, and the thunder rolls.

THOUGHTS OF A YOUNG MAN DYING IN THE SPRING

Tonight is a night of grasses in the wind.
Thunder and lightning and rain,
Warm drops of rain,
Watering the earth
Into an abundance of leaves,
Falling upon me, washing away
Tears of pain running to the earth.
Pain from the skies
Rains into the earth.
The earth absorbs all.

For we cannot suppose
That heaven is all happiness
With all these tears falling
In the thunder and lightning flashes
Of the skies; nor can we propose
That the water upon my eye-lashes
Is not some measure of my joy
In some fond memory of the sun
Of yesterday, when all the earth was green,
When all the earth is coming green again,

Here, in the thunder and lightning and rain.
The earth does not live not without purpose.
The morning and evening birds that sing
And trees that start their blossoming,
Or the clouds that float above
Dancing, graceful, rising from the earth,
Show me there is a love
Of the earth for its people
As loudly as the bell that rings

In the nearest church yard steeple.

And perhaps the rains from the sky
Are the tears of the angels who cry
Not in tears, but in remembering joy
Of having lived here once,
As I in joy cry to the sun
Coming in the red-skied east,
Shining into me, between the grasses
And the dawn-hushed wind,
Drying the grass to green.

COMPASSION

O! if you could know
What pain will come
From a word uttered without restraint
Because of some small complaint
In your heart or mind or soul
To interrupt the bliss of day
And jovial quietude.

I hurt when words unspoken
Or spoken by the face or tongue
Are harsh and sharp,
Thrown from the mind
Like a rock
Against a clear pool
Of sun's reflected waters,
Broken limply outwardly concentric
To the shore shadowed under by trees
In darkness now destroyed
By a word or thought,
Like bits of glasses tangled
In the roots of some odious root,
To bleed out, break and burst
And frame the structure of the heart
Against such hurting words again.

TO BEAUTY

O, moon that rose
This fair afternoon
As the motion of delight
Within me,
I feel thy tug carry me aloft
And loosen my delight and joy,
Haply moving the sky
To dusk and stillness,
Till quietly the darkness comes
To define thee.
Thy rays are pleasant waves
And flow of tidal seasons

With power to quell emotions.
I move with thee, moon,
Into lights and sights
That still the stars to stop,
Till all too soon
Down over the treetops
Like a big tear shed
Thou plunge out of sight
And thy soft light
Is taken from the night.

SPRING

Last night in six feet of snow
I heard a sparrow sing
Of sun in dew of spring.
I stroked the soft leaves
Outside my window
And saw the sparrow
Adjust himself on the bough,
Blink his eyes and flutter.
Then, not quite believing the reality
Of this small bird's conviviality,
With twigs and leaves
Still clinging to my bare thighs
Wet from the cold grass dew,
I crawled into bed once more
To sleep myself into
twigs and new leaves.

THE WHITE BIRD DREAM

In the cold chaos of time
When there was only endless night,
The ocean's water rolled on the lime—
Stone beginning of the Earth,
Cut into the solemn silent stone,
Where there was only boundless sea
And earth and starless sky—
The sound of a hushed sigh.

From the great breast of the earth
The small beginning of life
Whispered in warmth of desire,
An anguished feeling for fire
That cut like a hot piercing knife
Through the rivers of her black bed.
But nothing there was to gather
The sky into the lonely rivers.
In starless night, nothing delivers.

Without warning appeared
An eye, embryonic, omnipotent,
To set the sky aflame.
At that moment, a beast—
Primeval man—untamed
Appeared with the flame of the sun,
And the waters washed back from the land,
And the man, born of warmth,
Saw a white bird in flight above him;
Man, sun, bird, sky
And the water, and the cry
Of the bird above
And the man below
Still growing with the energy of love.

Here stood the new child
Of the Earth and Sky, their lineage.
Free, innocent, and wild,
Mysteriously created
In a great light stream.
And in his eyes, a gleam
Showed how innocent he was
As he began to walk
Upon the long beach,
Not yet in possession
Of a tongue to give him speech,
But only walked in joy
And harmony and peace
That never seemed to cease;
There was nothing to destroy
The gentleness of this calm beast,
A noble creature in his wildness.

Still alone, alone was I
In the motion of the bird's wings
That beat against the sky,
In the motion of illimitable space.
I walked along the seashore
Watching the white bird soar.
Softly as the wind touched my face
I opened my eyes to the blue dome
Watching the white bird fly
Over hot tickling sand,
Then settle near the brook.
And it was the white bird and I
Alone on the shore of our beginning
Before there was thought
Between the great depths of ocean and sky.

The bird's wings shone in the sunlight,
Quivering faintly from the long flight.
A long song started: a harmony.
I touched the white celestial bird
And note after throbbing note
Came from the trembling throat
Before there was fear.

Here was I in my waking dream
When the bird sang in the tree
In the waking dawn of the sun.
No mad pursuit or stifling strife
Nor plowing the empty field
Nor knife to wield against a brother;
No. God, this was not meant to be
Me, as I within my heart-strings looked
To watch him stroke his wings, white
In the brightness of the sunlight,
And preen himself and flutter
And in his deep throat utter
Another note, long and sonorous,
Then stopped, but his eyes were not onerous
Or mocking, as he spread his wings
And flapping them into the sun still glittering
Slowly rose from the bush, the bird
Flew away into the sky, another note unheard,
Flew away into the sun
Leaving me, my life, to be begun.
So, looking for water I strolled along the shore
And, walking alone, came upon an open door.

All good dreams are broken
Before they are spoken.

So it was with the lady in the grove
And the serpent that wove
His body round hers and brought her down
To the leaves on the ground,
The red apple rolling away.
She saw the man and wondered
At the broken sky which thundered.
The young man in the clearing
Far away from the hearing
Of words he might have heard
(But to him they'd have sounded absurd).
Light of the whispering trees
Mingling caresses of the breeze,
Invited the young man in,
Though it was less of a sin
Their fall together
Soft as drifting feather
Back to the sound of waves,
Echoes in hollow caves
On the seashore that circled round
The trees, and man and woman found
Like rivulets and milk-white streams
More delicate than flowery dreams.
The lovers slept the evening full,
Until the sun began to pull
Their eyes awake to consciousness,
Discovering them in their nakedness,
While the snake shed his skin
And slithered through the grass.

I sat on the edge of the green meadow
Where I had come to learn and know.
Near the river on an open stone

I sat and pondered, quietly, alone
I know it could have been more
Than just an open wound and war
Between God and man,
God and water and sand,
More than sun and the sky
Only to live and only to die
Sweeping sands of the vast desert,
A stillness that does not last.
We are all doomed to drown
In the visions that surround
Our starry moon-filled past
For having dreamed to forget.
We gained the knowledge of the sun
And felt the pleasure of our fun.
Was it so wrong to find our sight
Or wrong for day to kiss the night?

But as the earth is doomed to pain
To die and bloom and die again
So are we, mortals chained to the earth
By a bond of fate and birth
To rain which falls upon our tender flesh,
Upon the man, a rebel, cold and fresh
Along the ancient river of a dream
Breaking upon a rock downstream.
And the man whose mind sees paradise
Awakes with an image of a bird in his eyes.

CPSIA information can be obtained
at www.ICGtesting.com
Printed in the USA
FSHW010417160321